REPTILES

Q2AMedia

Created by Q2AMedia
www.q2amedia.com
Text, design & illustrations Copyright © 2008 Q2AMedia

Editor Honor Head
Publishing Director Chester Fisher
Art Director Sumit Charles
Senior Designers Joita Das
Project Managers Ravneet Kaur and Shekhar Kapur

Illustrators Subhash Vohra, Aadil A. Siddiqui and Amit Tayal
Art Editor Sujatha Menon
Picture Researcher Shweta Saxena

Tangerine Press edition Copyright © 2008 Scholastic Inc.

Scholastic and Tangerine Press and associated logos are trademarks of Scholastic Inc.

Published by Tangerine Press, an imprint of Scholastic Inc., 557 Broadway, New York, NY 10012

Scholastic New Zealand Ltd.
Greenmount, Auckland

Scholastic Canada Ltd.
Markham, Ontario

Scholastic Australia Pty. Ltd
Gosford NSW

Scholastic UK
Coventry, Warwickshire

10 9 8 7 6 5 4 3 2 1

ISBN-10: 0-545-08483-0
ISBN-13: 978-0-545-08483-3

Printed in China

Picture Credits
Cover Images:
Front: Q2AMedia, tl walkingmoon: Istockphoto, tm: David Davis: Shutterstock, tr: Brad Thompson: Shutterstock.

Back: Michael Lustbader:Photolibrary

Imprint: l: Vova Pomortzeff: Shutterstock, r:Michael Lustbader:Photolibrary,

Preliminary tl Pixelpipe: Istockphoto. tr Clint Spencer's Photography: Istockphoto. bl John Bell: Shutterstock. br Steve Lovegrove: Shutterstock.

6-7 Bob Blanchard: Shutterstock. 7t Chen Ping Hung/Shutterstock. 7b Irmine: Bigstockphoto, Jessica Bethke: Shutterstock, Lucian: Istockphoto, Harryfn: Dreamstime, Steve Lovegrove: Shutterstock, John Billingslea jr.: Istockphoto,

Eric Isselée: Istockphoto, Pilar Echeverria: Istockphoto, John Bell: Shutterstock, Dejan Sarman: Dreamstine, Clint Spencer's Photography: Istockphoto 8 Tom Antos: Shutterstock. 10-11 Suzi Eszterhas: GettyImages. 11t ASSOCIATED PRESS. 12-13 Anup Shah: Naturepl.com. 12t Mark Deeble & Victoria Stone: Oxford Scientific (OSF): Photolibrary. 13t Michael Fogden: Oxford Scientific (OSF): Photolibrary. 13b Nicole Duplaix: GettyImages. 14 Tim Laman: GettyImages. 16-17 Belinda Wright: Oxford Scientific (OSF): Photolibrary. 16t ZIGMUND LESZCZYNSKI: Animals Animals: Photolibrary. 17t: Stephen Dalton: NHPA. 18 TED MEAD: Photolibrary. 19t Tim Flach: GettyImages. 19b John Cancalosi: Naturepl.com. 21t Mark A. Johnson / Alamy. 22 Bruce Farnsworth: Alamy. 23 BRECK P KENT: Animals Animals: Photolibrary. 24-25 Nature Production: Naturepl.com. 24t Robert Valentic: Naturpl.com. 25t Anthony Bannister: NHPA. 26 CHRIS

MATTISON: NHPA. 27t C Allan Morgan: Photolibrary. 27b Pending. 28 PHOTO RESEARCHERS: Photolibrary. 30t Jerry Young: GettyImages. 30b Karl H Switak: Photolibrary. 31 Michael D. Kern: Naturepl.com. 32t blickwinkel: Alamy. 32b JOE BLOSSOM: NHPA. 33 Lorraine Swanson: Shutterstock. 34 SUPERSTOCK INC: Photolibrary . 36-37 Gregory Ochocki: Photolibrary. 36t STEPHEN DALTON: NHPA. 37t DANIEL HEUCLIN: NHPA. 38-39 Ingo Arndt: Naturepl.com. 38t Tim Laman/National Geographic Image Collection: National Geographic. 41t Rodney Lewis. 42-43 Michael & Patricia Fogden: GettyImages. 43t TIM MARTIN: Naturepl.com. 44 Rodney Lewis. 45t Eric Isselée: Shutterstock. 45b: Nicole Duplaix: GettyImages. 46-47 Ken Griffiths: NHPA. 47t Snowleopard1: Shutterstock.

Index: Zina Seletskaya: Shutterstock

REPTILES

Tom Jackson

tangerine press

an imprint of
■SCHOLASTIC

Contents

Alligator

Rattlesnake

Snapping turtle

Feel the Squeeze

Mighty boa constrictors and pythons are deadly creatures that squeeze their prey to death and then swallow it whole. They can open their mouths wide to eat animals almost twice their size.

Perfect Poisoners

Some of the world's most feared reptiles are snakes that have venom powerful enough to kill a human. They can target their poison with deadly accuracy.

Armor-Plated

Turtles and tortoises have been around for more than 250 million years and have developed cunning ways to survive in all habitats, including scorching deserts and under the water.

Facts and Records

Data, record-breakers, and fascinating facts.

Glossary and Threatened Species

Index

Thorny devil

What are Reptiles?

Reptiles come in many shapes, sizes, and colors. Some of the smallest are no bigger than your hand; others are massive. Most are harmless, while others are master killers.

The same but different

There are nearly 8,000 species of reptiles alive today in all parts of the world. Reptiles include lizards, snakes, alligators, crocodiles, and turtles. Whatever type they are, reptiles share a few things. They have skin covered in hard scales, they shed their skin as they grow, and their babies develop inside eggs.

NORTH AMERICA

Atlantic Ocean

Pacific Ocean

SOUTH AMERICA

▶| *A male anole lizard flaps a red dewlap, or chin crest, to attract females. If a rival male gets too close, the lizard will scare it away with a display of push-ups.*

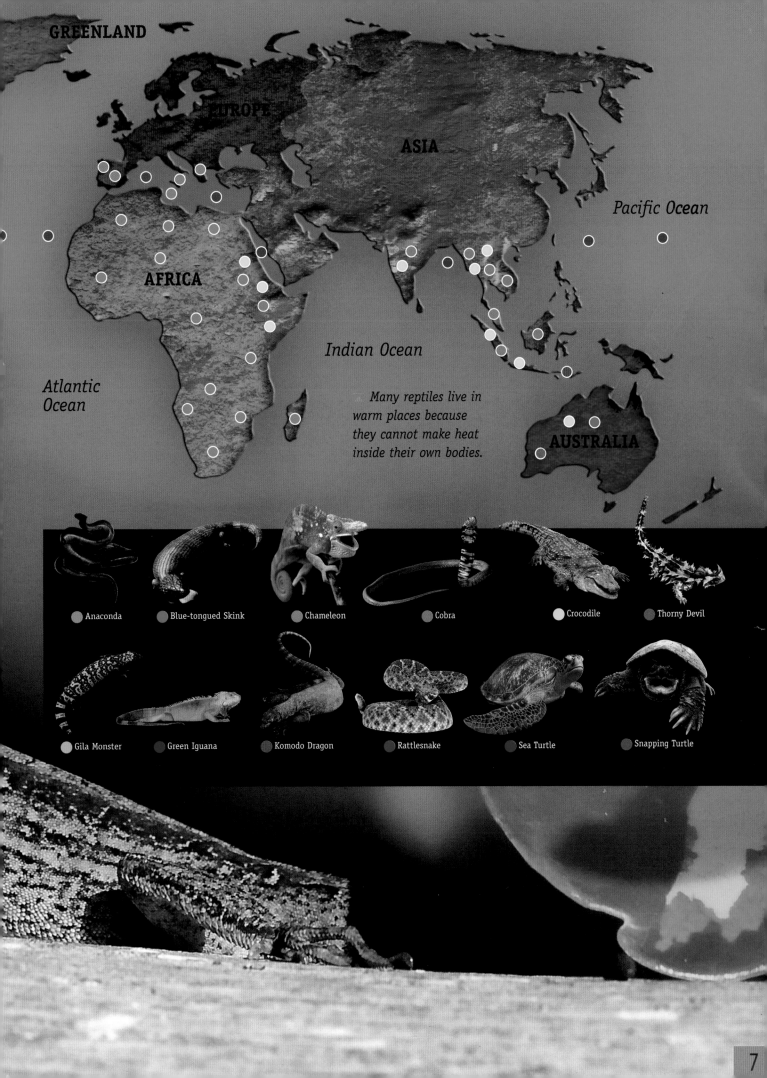

GREENLAND

EUROPE

ASIA

Pacific Ocean

AFRICA

Indian Ocean

Atlantic
Ocean

Many reptiles live in
warm places because
they cannot make heat
inside their own bodies.

AUSTRALIA

● Anaconda   ● Blue-tongued Skink   ● Chameleon   ● Cobra   ○ Crocodile   ● Thorny Devil

● Gila Monster   ● Green Iguana   ● Komodo Dragon   ● Rattlesnake   ● Sea Turtle   ● Snapping Turtle

Deadly Hunters

Crocodiles are armor-plated killing machines. They have been terrorizing their prey in steamy swamps and murky rivers for more than 200 million years.

Super reptiles

Crocodiles are the world's largest reptiles. These giant killers have been hunting in the world's rivers and shallow seas since before the dinosaurs roamed the earth. No other river animal has come close to matching crocodiles for strength and speed.

◀ *Crocodiles have eyes and nostrils on the top of their head so they can hide in muddy water but still see and breathe.*

Hunting and fishing

Crocodiles mainly live in the world's warm, wet places and prey on fish, birds, antelopes, and other large land animals. The largest crocodiles are found in the salty seas around Southeast Asia and Australia. These monster crocs can grow to more than 22 feet (7 m)—the length of a small yacht.

Bony plates called scutes give the tail a paddle shape for swimming.

The scutes cover the body for protection against predators. They are thickest at the neck.

The legs are short, so the crocodile moves by wriggling on its belly. But it can also stand up on its legs and run.

The snout is long and V-shaped.

Sharp teeth are used for stabbing into prey and ripping off chunks of flesh.

When its mouth is closed, the upper and lower teeth poke out at the side.

Long claws help the croc grip the ground.

Ambush killers

Crocodiles hunt at the water's edge. They lie in wait, hidden by the water, for animals to come to the bank to drink. The killer reptile glides silently toward its prey before lunging forward with a flick of its tail. It grabs its startled prey in its mighty jaws. If the first bite does not kill it, the victim is dragged underwater until it drowns.

Chunky food

Crocodiles cannot chew their food. They swallow it whole. With bigger prey, they twist chunks off by grabbing their victim and rolling around until the flesh rips off. This is called a death roll. Crocodiles swallow pebbles, too. These stones help grind up the food.

▶| *During the wildebeest migration in Africa, hundreds of thousands of the animals wade across a river in Kenya. Many end up as crocodile food.*

FACT

Crocodiles have a third eyelid, which moves sideways across each eye. These eyelids are see-through and act like a pair of goggles in the water.

Open wide

Crocodiles have a powerful bite—strong enough to take a chunk out of a boat! However, only the muscles used to close the mouth are strong. The ones that open it are very weak. Some crocodile hunters and experts can hold a croc's mouth shut with their hands.

▶️ *A crocodile swallows a chunk of food whole by throwing its head back and letting the food slide down its throat.*

Baby crocodiles

Crocodiles lay their eggs in nests made from mud and dead grass. When the baby crocodiles are hatching, they chirp to call their mother back to the nest. The mother helps her hatchlings by digging them out of the nest and carrying them to the water.

Boy or girl—hot or cold?

The eggs at the top and bottom of the nest normally hatch into females. Eggs in the middle become males. That's because a crocodile's sex is decided by the temperature of the nest—medium temperatures produce males, while high or low temperatures produce females.

◄ A crocodile mother can be very gentle, carefully watching out for her babies. She might carry her babies in her mouth or give them a ride on her back.

What's a croc?

There are 23 types of crocodile species living around the world today. Although they all look similar, they are different animals. The strangest-looking of all is the gharial. A male gharial has a hollow lump, or "pot," on its snout. He uses his pot to blow bubbles in the water and make buzzing noises to attract females.

An alligator has a wider, more rounded snout. Only the upper teeth are visible when its mouth is closed.

Super Lizards!

Many of the most amazing lizards are from the iguana family. Some can almost fly, others can run across water, and some can change colors.

Walking on water

Basilisks are little iguanas from the jungles of Central America. They spend most of their time hunting for insects in the branches of trees. But when it's under attack, the basilisk leaps to the ground and runs on its back legs for the safety of a pond or stream. Instead of diving in, the lizard just keeps on running across the surface of the water.

Forest flyer

The flying lizard has a pair of wings made from skin stretched over its long ribs. When the lizard is crawling up a tree, the rib-wings are tucked away. But when it's time to move to another tree, the lizard raises its ribs and glides through the air. The undersides of a male flying lizard's wings are blue. He spreads his wings open and closed to impress the females.

Flying lizards do not actually fly. They glide from tree to tree on flaps of skin.

The tail is used to balance the lizard as it runs on two legs.

A male basilisk has a plume of scaly skin on its head. The males with the biggest plumes attract the most females.

Crests on the tail and back are used as paddles when the lizard finally sinks into the water.

Long toes distribute the lizard's weight evenly so it can run over the water's surface.

15

To win a mate, a male chameleon needs territory. This pair of male Jackson's chameleons is jousting to see which one will take control of the branch.

Color coded

The chameleons are among the most well known of all lizards because they can change color. The color change is a form of camouflage, which helps the chameleon blend in with its surroundings. They also use colors and patterns to let each other know how they are feeling and to warn off any attackers.

Frightening frills

When disturbed, the feisty little frilled lizard runs at its attacker with a large umbrella of skin unfolded into a frill around its head. The frill is as wide as the lizard is long and makes the lizard look much bigger.

These frilled lizards try to scare each other away by showing off their wide neck frills.

▶| *A chameleon unleashes its long, sticky tongue to capture a grasshopper. The chameleon uses its prehensile, or wrap-around, tail to cling onto a branch.*

FACT

Iguanas on the rocky San Fernandina Island in the Pacific bury their eggs in the crater of a volcano because that's the only place with soil soft enough to dig into.

Spikes for life

Many reptiles that live in deserts don't drink much—they get the water they need from their food. However, the thorny devil has a clever trick. It uses spikes on its back and tail to collect dew. Tiny droplets of water form on the spikes each morning, and they trickle along grooves between the skin scales that lead to the mouth.

The thorny devil's spikes not only provide water, but they also make the lizard difficult for a predator to eat.

Poison lizard

The Gila monster is one of only two kinds of lizard that has a venomous bite. The venom, or poison, is in the lizard's spit and gets into the wounds of its prey when it attacks. The Gila monster catches the prey in its powerful jaws and won't let go until the poison has taken effect.

▲ *Gila monsters hunt by tasting or smelling the air with their tongue for the scent of their prey.*

▼ *The Texas horned lizard has a scary way of warding off attackers: It squirts blood at them from its eyes! Sometimes it even gets blood on its face.*

The Komodo Dragon

The largest and fiercest of all lizards is the Komodo dragon, which is a monitor lizard. This monster has a deadly bite and a big appetite.

Real-life monster

Komodo dragons grow to 10 feet (3 m) long. Komodos live on a few small islands in Indonesia, where they terrorize prey such as wild pigs and even buffaloes. Komodo dragons can kill with a single bite. Their spit is full of nasty germs that get into the victim's blood. It might take a while, but eventually the prey dies from infection. Komodo dragons have big appetites; they can eat half their body weight in a single meal.

Long claws help to burrow and climb up tree trunks.

Komodo dragons have powerful tails they use to club their victims and to paddle when swimming.

Wrestling champs

The goanna is the biggest monitor lizard in Australia—reaching 3 feet (1 m) in length. These monitors are from the same family as Komodo dragons. All monitor lizards can stand upright on their back legs and use their tail for support.

▶| *Goannas often end up in a fight over territory or a mate. The lizards wrestle face to face and try to push their opponents over.*

Sharp teeth are used to rip off flesh.

Komodo dragons can walk with their body raised off the ground.

Scuttle and Scurry

Geckos and skinks are the smallest lizards. Geckos can scurry up walls and across ceilings. Skinks slip unseen through the undergrowth.

▶| *Whiptails, such as this rainbow whiptail, are an unusual type of skink. Some whiptail species are all female and can produce young without a male.*

Squeaky geckos

The colorful tokay is the largest type of gecko. It's as long as a man's forearm. It gets its name from its squeaky, quack-like calls that male tokays make to attract females. Male tokays make this call to attract females. And if a young tokay or smaller male gets too close, the big male will eat it up!

Wiggle and slither

Skinks are longer and thinner than geckos. They have a very long tail that's almost twice as long as the rest of their body. Skinks like to hide in long grass and under leaves. They wiggle their body and tail so they can slither around in the undergrowth without using their legs.

The gecko's toe pads stick to flat surfaces so they can hang upside-down. The pads have many folds so there's a lot of skin to cling on to the surface.

Tokays kill with a crushing bite.

Tokays have no eyelids and cannot blink. They lick their eyes clean with their tongue.

⊻ Tokay

Sticking out its tongue

The blue-tongued skink is a common sight in Australia. It often wanders into gardens in search of food, where it gobbles down snails and insects as well as flowers and fruits. It's not afraid to meet people. When scared, the skink rolls out its wide, blue tongue. This flash of color scares off most attackers. If not, the big skink gives them a painful nip.

The skink flashes its blue tongue at attackers and also gives a warning hiss.

Tell tail

Skinks have a special way to escape predators. If something grabs them by the tail, it falls off. The lizard has special bones at the base of the tail that can make a clean break. The lost tail wriggles and writhes to keep the attacker looking as the tailless lizard dashes away to safety. A new tail will grow back, but it will never be as long as the first.

Circle of spikes

The armadillo lizard is covered in heavily armored spikes. When it's attacked, this skink rolls itself up and tucks the tip of its tail into its mouth.

▶ | *The armadillo lizard can turn itself into a coil of spikes so that a predator will not be able to attack or bite it.*

⬱ *This skink's tail is brightly colored so attackers can see it better than the more important part of its body.*

Hiding out

Most geckos are climbing lizards, which can cause a big problem—the lizard's shadow under its body makes it easy for predators to spot it. Leaf-tailed geckos have solved the problem. They have a flat flap that bulges out of each side of the tail and a frill of spines around the body that stop the give-away shadows from forming.

The leaf-tailed gecko has very clever camouflage. Can you spot it?

Lonely reptile

Tuataras might look like lizards, but they are a completely different type of reptile. Tuataras lived during the time of the dinosaurs, long before lizards and snakes arrived. Today, there are hardly any left. A few thousand live only on small islands in New Zealand. They live for a long time—perhaps 100 years. Attempts to breed more tuataras have not been very successful. It takes almost a year for one of their eggs to hatch.

Big feet

Web-footed geckos live in the Namib Desert in Namibia and Angola. It is difficult to walk on loose sand, so these geckos have wide, webbed feet that stop them from sinking into the ground. It's too hot above ground in the day, so the geckos paddle into the sand to stay cool. They come out to feed at night when it's cooler, and they drink the water that forms on their skin. When the skink feels scared, it stands tall on stiff legs to try and look bigger.

The skin of web-footed geckos is so thin you can see the blood vessels underneath.

27

Feel the Squeeze

The world's largest snakes kill by wrapping themselves around their prey and squeezing the victim to death with their coiled bodies. These snakes are called constrictors.

Green giant

The largest constrictors are pythons and boas. The biggest of all is a monster boa known as the green anaconda. This giant grows to 32 feet (10 m) long and weighs a quarter of a ton (tonne). Some pythons have grown longer, but few are as big and strong as an anaconda. These fearless snakes hunt in rivers and swamps, and they're afraid of nothing—they even attack crocodiles and jaguars!

Great but small

Not all constricting snakes are giants. Most of them are snakes that make up the colubrid family and are only about 3 feet (1 m) long. They include common grass snakes, milk snakes, and corn snakes. Many in this group of snakes are exactly the same species but look totally different because they have different skin colors and patterns. This helps them to blend in with where they live and hide from enemies.

These corn snakes kill by squeezing their prey to death. Their different colors and patterns are part of their camouflage and mimicry.

The windpipe opens at the front of the mouth so the snake can breathe even with its mouth full.

The eyes are on top of the head so they stay above the water when the snake swims.

Small teeth are razor-sharp hooks. They stop a victim from struggling free if it's not completely dead when it's being swallowed.

Anacondas have a wide mouth so they can swallow even armored prey, like a caiman.

The mighty coils don't crush the victim's body. Instead, they are gradually tightened until the prey can no longer breathe.

Tasting the air

A snake's forked tongue is used not only for tasting, but also to smell. The snake flicks its tongue in and out to pick up the scent of prey in the air. Scents stick to the tips of the tongue. Inside the mouth, the tongue tips are pushed into slots in the top of the mouth, where the scents are recognized.

◂ *If one tip of the fork picks up more of a scent than the other, the snake knows the source must be in that direction.*

Big mouth

Snakes can't chew or bite, so they have to swallow their prey whole. That's not easy when a victim is larger than the snake's head! A snake gets around this by opening its mouth really wide. Once the mouth is opened, the snake does not pull food down its throat—it slowly slides its body around the prey until its body surrounds it.

◂ *Egg-eating snakes have to stretch their mouths wider than most species. The snake's backbone cuts into the shell as the egg is swallowed, so it cracks open in the stomach.*

Heat seekers

Many snakes have heat sensors that allow them to hunt at night. Snakes cannot see prey in the dark, but with their heat sensors, that is not a problem. The sensors are hollows, or pits, on their face, which can detect body heat, like a set of night-vision goggles. These heat sensors even work through leaves, so the snakes can find prey hiding in a bush.

▶︎ *This green tree python has pits along its upper lip. These heat sensors are only used to find warm-blooded prey like rats and birds. They would not be able to find most cold-blooded prey, like other reptiles.*

⏶ *A carpet python is coiled around her eggs. The mother does not eat while she protects her eggs, but she might take a break in the sunshine so she doesn't get too cold.*

Shivering shelter

A python makes a good mother. Once she has laid her eggs, she wraps herself around them to keep them safe. Now and then, she shivers her muscles. The heat made by the twitching muscles warms the eggs until they are ready to hatch.

Playing dead

If a grass snake is attacked, it plays dead. It coils up and lies with its tongue out and mouth open. Predators like to eat fresh meat, so they'll leave animals alone that are already dead. Once the predator has gone, the grass snake comes back to "life."

◀ *As well as playing dead, grass snakes also pump a smelly liquid from their bottoms when threatened, so they not only look unappetizing but smell bad, too.*

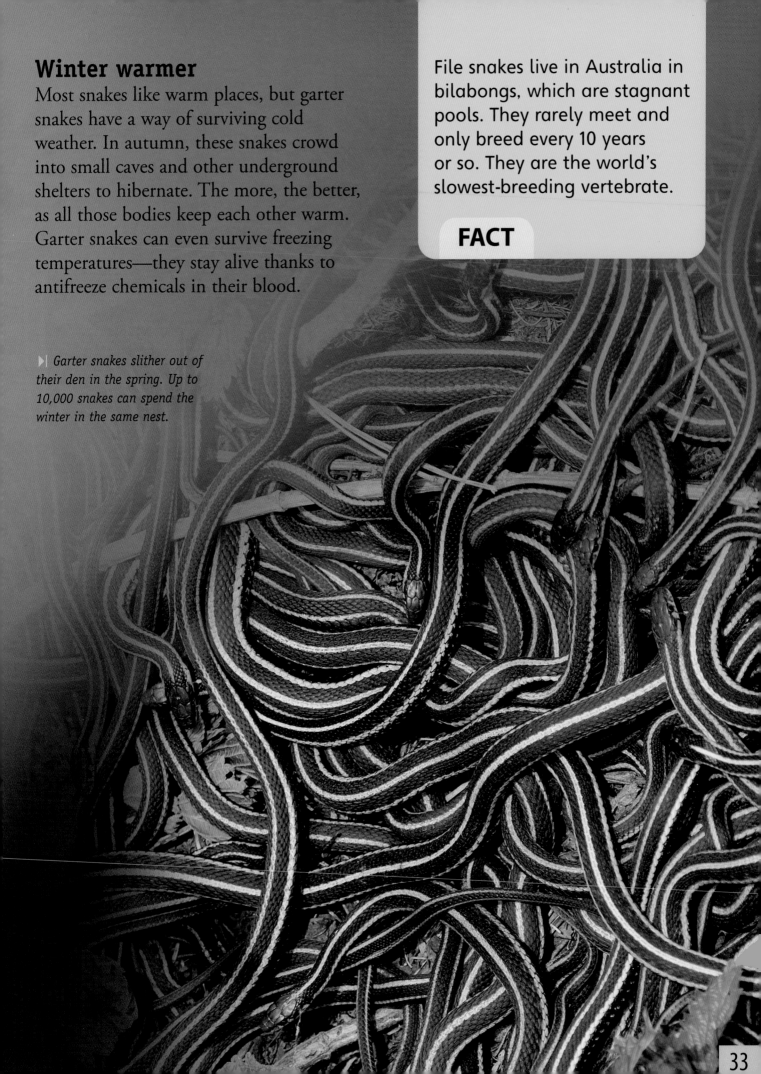

Winter warmer

Most snakes like warm places, but garter snakes have a way of surviving cold weather. In autumn, these snakes crowd into small caves and other underground shelters to hibernate. The more, the better, as all those bodies keep each other warm. Garter snakes can even survive freezing temperatures—they stay alive thanks to antifreeze chemicals in their blood.

▶ *Garter snakes slither out of their den in the spring. Up to 10,000 snakes can spend the winter in the same nest.*

File snakes live in Australia in bilabongs, which are stagnant pools. They rarely meet and only breed every 10 years or so. They are the world's slowest-breeding vertebrate.

FACT

33

Perfect Poisoners

Some venomous snakes can kill a human with a single bite. The snakes pump venom (poison) into the victim, which can shut down the body.

Deadly spit

The venom of poisonous snakes is filled with powerful chemicals that can stop the victim's body from working properly. Some snake venom attacks the nerves, making it impossible for a victim to move or breathe. Other venom attacks the blood, and the victim bleeds on the inside.

Kill or be killed

Most venomous snakes use their venom to kill the animals they hunt for food. However, they can use their venom to defend themselves, too. Some snakes make super-powerful venom. A single bite from a king cobra can kill a human within about 30 minutes.

◄ *When they're under attack, king cobras lift their head off the ground and flatten their ribs into a "hood." This is a signal that they're about to bite.*

Shield-shaped scales
overlap each other.

The head is arrow-shaped
to fit large bags of poison
behind each eye.

Fangs hang down
from the front of
the mouth. With
some snakes, when
the fangs are not
in use, they're
folded against the
roof of the mouth.

This is the opening
to the windpipe.

When not in use, the
forked tongue is hidden
inside this fleshy sheath.

Biting snakes such as this
temple viper lunge forward with
lightning speed to grab prey or
sink their teeth into an attacker.

Warning signs

Venom is precious stuff, and snakes don't want to waste it. Rattlesnakes use a rattle on their tails to warn other animals not to get too close. The rattle is made from dried skin. Each time the snake sheds its skin, it leaves a button of old skin on the rattle. Over the years, this builds up into a long rattle that has a terrifying clatter.

⌅ A rattlesnake rattles a warning with its tail. The older the snake, the longer the rattle will be.

Water hunters

Several venomous snakes hunt in water and on land, but the yellow-bellied sea snake spends its entire life at sea. The snake's tail is flattened into a paddle to help it swim. It breathes air but can dive to 492 feet (150 m). The snake's body is so well built for life in water that it can't move across land.

▷| Sea kraits hunt around coral reefs for eels and small fish. They spend most of their time at sea, but climb into caves along the shoreline to lay their eggs.

A whip snake has keyhole-shaped pupils so it can scan a wide area of forest, but still see straight ahead.

On target

A whip snake needs to have a great aim to hit fast-moving prey such as frogs, small birds, and lizards. It has a pointed snout with grooves on it that lines up with the target. The snake's venom works very fast, and the prey dies before it gets too far.

◄ *Despite its name, the flying snake really glides.*

Flying without wings

The golden tree snake is sometimes called the flying snake because it makes huge leaps across gaps in trees. The snake spreads its ribs to make a curved "wing" that catches the air.

A sideways move

It's almost impossible to slither across loose sand. The sidewinder, a desert snake, has solved this problem with a whole new way of moving around. Its body forms a curve in the same way as other species, only instead of pushing forward, the snake lifts sections of its body off the ground and throws them to the side. In that way, it crosses the sand without having to really touch it.

▶ *Sidewinders leave a pattern in the sand as they shimmy across it.*

Push and pull

It's surprising how many ways a snake can move. The familiar slithering action happens when snakes form their body into several curves. The snake's belly is covered with hook-shaped scales that anchor it to the ground. As the curve shapes move down a snake's body like a wave, each part of the body pushes against the ground and makes the snake move forward.

Concertina

Sidewinding

Serpentine

Caterpillar

Armor-Plated

Turtles and tortoises are the oldest type of reptiles alive today. They have been around for more than 250 million years and are the only reptiles that have a shell.

The sharp, bony beak has two huge points, which cut right through a victim's body.

Finger snapper

The largest type of river turtle is the fierce-looking alligator snapping turtle. It rarely comes onto land. Instead, the turtle sits on the muddy bottom and waits for prey to come by. The turtle can eat almost anything thanks to its beak, which is strong enough to bite through most things—including fingers!

The tongue tip looks like a fleshy worm. The turtle wiggles this "bait" to attract fish.

The turtle sits motionless underwater with its mouth open. It can stay like this for 45 minutes before needing to breathe.

Bone safe

In general, turtles live in water, both rivers and the sea, while tortoises are land-based reptiles. Tortoises are known for being slow and lumbering. They're kept safe by their protective shells made of flat bones that are fused together.

▶| *A tortoise shell is covered by huge scales, called scutes. This leopard tortoise has ridged bulges to strengthen the shell.*

Claws are used to dig a hole for the eggs a short distance away from the water's edge.

The turtle is motionless for so much of the time that algae and weeds sometimes grow on its spiked shell.

Snorkel snout

The matamata is a truly strange-looking turtle. It lives in the creeks of the Amazon jungle. A matamata has long, flexible nostrils, which it pokes out of the surface of the water to take a breath. Matamatas have wide mouths inside triangular heads. They catch prey, such as little fish, by opening their mouths very wide and sucking in their victims.

▼ *The frills around the matamata's head are highly sensitive and can pick up currents in the water made by prey.*

FACT

Most turtles must come to the surface of the water every now and then to breathe air, but one species from Australia gets oxygen from the water. The Fitzroy-River turtle absorbs oxygen into its blood through its bottom!

Soft and smooth

The largest turtle of all is the mighty leatherback. This deep-sea turtle has a soft, flexible shell and grows to an enormous size—it's 9 feet (3 m) long and the same across when it has its fins stretched out. The long fins make the turtle an excellent swimmer. The leatherback eats almost nothing but jellyfish. It has spikes in its throat to burst open its victim's body and stop the prey from swimming back out of its mouth.

▲ Female leatherbacks struggle up a beach to lay their eggs in a hole. Once they have finished and filled in the hole, the turtles drag themselves around the top in a circle to hide their work.

Facts and Records

Record-breakers

The smallest reptile of all is a gecko called the Jaragua Sphaero. This tiny creature lives on a few Caribbean islands. It is only 0.5 inch (16 mm) long from the head to the tip of the tail — not much longer than a fingernail.

The smallest snake also lives in the Caribbean. The thread snake grows to about 3 inches (10 cm) long and is as narrow as a pencil lead.

The fastest-running reptile is the spiny-tailed iguana of Costa Rica. It can travel at 20 mph (33 kph). Without any legs, the fastest snake cannot match that speed, but the black mamba is capable of slithering at 12 mph (20 kph). That's about as fast as a person can run! The fastest reptile of all travels in water. The leatherback turtle swims at 21 mph (35 kph).

A giant tortoise can live for up to 200 years.

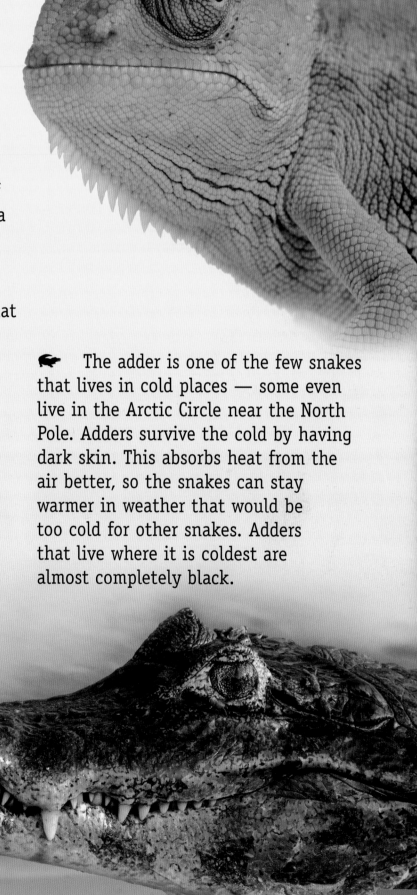

▶| *A chameleon can roll each eye in a different direction. This means it can look for food or predators in two places at the same time.*

Reptile facts

🐊 Not all reptiles lay their eggs. Many types of lizards and snakes give birth to live young. The females keep their eggs inside their body instead of laying them in a nest. The eggs have a shell, and once the baby reptiles have hatched, they wriggle out of their mother. Boa constrictors and rattlesnakes are two types of snake that give birth like this.

🐊 In addition to lizards, snakes, turtles, and crocodiles, there is one other large group of reptiles — the worm lizards. Although these look like narrow snakes and have the word "lizard" in their name, they are a completely different type of animal.

🐊 Most worm lizards have no legs. They live underground, where they eat insects and worms. Worm lizards hardly ever come to the surface.

🐊 The adder is one of the few snakes that lives in cold places — some even live in the Arctic Circle near the North Pole. Adders survive the cold by having dark skin. This absorbs heat from the air better, so the snakes can stay warmer in weather that would be too cold for other snakes. Adders that live where it is coldest are almost completely black.

▶| *A crocodile may have about 60 teeth in its mouth at one time. As a tooth falls out, it's replaced by a new one.*

Glossary

Camouflage The patterns on an animal's skin that help it blend in with its surroundings so enemies cannot see it. Many reptiles are green and brown so they can hide in bushes and in leaves on the ground.

Droughts A time when there in no rain and the ground becomes very dry. Rivers and lakes dry out quickly when there is a drought, and animals and plants find it harder to survive.

Jousting A way of fighting.

Migration A journey made by an animal to find food, water, or mates. Animals migrate to avoid cold or dry weather, too.

Mimicry When one animal pretends to be another species. Harmless snakes often mimic dangerous snakes so enemies are too scared to attack them.

Predator An animal that kills other animals for its food.

Prey An animal that is hunted for food by another animal. For example, mice are the prey of several types of snakes.

Species A group of animals or plants that are very similar to each other.

▶| *This carpet python is a predator. The animal it has eaten is its prey.*

Territory An area that is controlled by one animal or a group of animals. An animal will try to stop another animal from coming into its territory to steal its food or kill its young.

Venom A poison made by an animal, such as a snake, that is pumped or injected into another animal in order to kill it.

Venomous An animal that uses venom to kill prey or to defend itself.

Vertebrate An animal that has a backbone, or spine. Reptiles are a type of vertebrate. So are mammals (like humans), most fish, birds, and frogs.

⊼ *Giant tortoise*

Threatened species

Many reptiles are very rare and some will become extinct if nothing is done to save them. People often do not realize that reptiles are in danger – it seems odd that a huge crocodile or deadly snake might need our help, but many do. Many deadly snakes are rare because people kill them. Other reptiles are rare because they have lived in one habitat for many millions of years, and this habitat is now being destroyed.

Some of the rarest reptiles are:

Chinese alligator
Leatherback turtle
Round Island boa (snake)
Giant Hispaniolan galliwasp (skink)
Giant tortoises of the Galapagos Islands
Golden lancehead (snake)
Jamaica ground iguana

Index